For
Aunt Allie
+
Uncle
Rusty
Love Cir + HA

Delicious Holiday
Chocolate & Cookies

Compiled by Evelyn L. Beilenson

Illustrations by Joanna Roy
Book Design by Lesley Ehlers

 Peter Pauper Press, Inc.
White Plains, New York

To Ethel Mills, for her help in testing many of
the recipes herein, and for her friendship

Original illustrations copyright ©1998
Joanna Roy
Text copyright © 1998, 1999
Peter Pauper Press, Inc.
202 Mamaroneck Avenue
White Plains, NY 10601
All rights reserved
ISBN 0-88088-408-8
Printed in China
8 7 6 5 4 3 2

Our thanks to Barbara Bloch
for the introduction and seven of the recipes

Contents

Chocolate

Contents

Cookies

Chocolate

Chocolate Know-How

Not all chocolate is equal—the better the chocolate tastes, the more it is likely to cost. The usual cooking chocolate available in supermarkets is perfectly fine for family cooking. However, if you are cooking for company or making a treat to give as a gift, you may want to consider using the best chocolate you can afford.

The easiest way to melt chocolate is to break it up and place the pieces in a heavy saucepan over very low heat. Stir constantly and remove chocolate from the heat as soon as it has melted, or finish the melting process off heat. You can also melt chocolate in the top of a double boiler set over (not in) simmering water. Don't ever, under any circumstances, cover chocolate. If even one drop of water gets into the chocolate it will cause the chocolate to stiffen. Fortunately you can remedy the situation by adding 1 teaspoon of vegetable shortening (don't substitute butter) for every square of chocolate used. Chocolate can also be melted in a microwave oven. Place broken chocolate in a microsafe dish and cook on HIGH one or two minutes. Remember, don't cover it! Stir and cook an additional minute if necessary. No matter what method you use to melt chocolate, watch it carefully. Nothing can be done to rescue burnt

chocolate. If that happens, throw it out and start over.

When chocolate is stored in a place where the temperature may fluctuate, it may develop a gray film referred to as a "bloom." This does not mean the chocolate has gone bad. It can still be used and it will not have lost any flavor. To avoid this problem, store tightly-wrapped chocolate in the refrigerator but be sure to bring it to room temperature before using.

Most recipes that call for cocoa mean unsweetened cocoa. Dutch-processed cocoa has the best flavor. You can substitute cocoa for chocolate.

1 square chocolate = 1 ounce
3 tablespoons cocoa plus 1 tablespoon vegetable shortening =
    1 square unsweetened chocolate (add small amount of
    granulated sugar to taste for semisweet or sweet chocolate)
3 squares (3 ounces) semisweet chocolate = 3 ounces (1/2 cup)
    semisweet chocolate chips

Chocolate will not set properly if the humidity or temperature is high. Avoid working with chocolate on a rainy day and, if the weather is very hot, turn on the air conditioner.

Chocolate Truffles

3/4 cup heavy cream
8 ounces semisweet or dark sweet chocolate, coarsely chopped
2 tablespoons dark rum, brandy, Amaretto, or other liqueur (optional)

Choice of coatings:
Unsweetened cocoa
Chocolate sprinkles
Finely chopped almonds, pecans, or walnuts

Place cream in medium size heavy saucepan. Cook over moderate heat just until bubbles begin to form around edges of cream. Add chocolate and cook, stirring, about 2 minutes. Remove from heat and continue stirring until chocolate is completely melted. Cool to room temperature and stir in liqueur. Spoon into bowl, cover loosely with waxed paper, and chill in refrigerator at least 2 hours or until thickened, stirring occasionally.

Line cookie sheet with waxed paper. Dust hands lightly with confectioners sugar or cocoa. Form chocolate mixture into 1-inch balls and place balls on lined cookie sheet. Place cookie sheet, uncovered, in refrigerator at least ten minutes or until truffles are firm.

Line second cookie sheet with waxed paper and set aside. One coating may be used for all truffles or a variety of coatings may be used. Place each coating on separate piece of waxed paper and roll truffles gently in coating. Place coated truffles on freshly lined cookie sheet and return to refrigerator, uncovered, until firm.

When truffles are firm, place in miniature paper cups, if desired, and place between layers of waxed paper in tightly covered container. Store in refrigerator.

About 2 dozen truffles

Chocolate-Nut Crunch

1 cup sugar
1/2 cup unsalted butter
1/4 teaspoon salt
1 cup chopped nuts (walnuts or pecans), divided
6 squares (6 ounces) semisweet chocolate

Grease 15 x 10-inch cookie sheet and set aside. Place sugar, butter, salt, and 1/4 cup water in heavy saucepan. Cook over medium heat, stirring, until mixture reaches soft-ball stage (270° on candy thermometer). Stir 1/2 cup nuts into mixture and pour onto prepared cookie sheet. Spread with greased spatula to about 1/4-inch thickness and set aside until cool. Place chocolate in heavy saucepan and cook over low heat until melted. Spread melted chocolate over cooled nut mixture and sprinkle top with remaining 1/2 cup chopped nuts. Set aside until chocolate is firmly set. Break into irregular size pieces (as in peanut brittle).

Approximately 30 to 40 pieces

Chocolate Meringues

2 egg whites
3/4 cup confectioners sugar
1/2 tsp. vanilla
1/2 cup finely chopped walnuts
6 oz. semisweet chocolate, melted

Beat egg whites until soft peaks form. Beat in sugar, 1 tablespoonful at a time, until stiff and glossy. Add vanilla. Fold in nuts and chocolate. Drop by teaspoonfuls onto ungreased cookie sheets and bake in preheated 350° oven 10 minutes. Cool on racks. Serve with vanilla ice cream. (Caution: Do not make on rainy or humid day.)

About 3-1/2 dozen

Chocolate-Dipped Treasures

Treasures of your choice:
  washed and hulled large strawberries
  firm banana chunks
  pineapple wedges
  marshmallows
  miniature pretzels
  dried fruit
4 to 6 ounces (4 to 6 squares) semisweet chocolate

Line several cookie sheets with wax paper and set aside. Prepare fruit or other food to be dipped. Place chocolate in medium-size heavy saucepan and cook over low heat, stirring, until melted. Remove pan from heat. Using a fork, toothpicks, or skewers, dip food quickly into chocolate and place on waxed paper until chocolate is set.

Chocolate Mousse Cheesecake

Crust:
1 cup plain graham cracker crumbs (see note)
2 tablespoons unsweetened cocoa
3 tablespoons sugar
4 tablespoons unsalted butter, melted

Cheesecake:
6 squares (6 ounces) semisweet chocolate
1 envelope unflavored gelatin
1/4 cup warm milk
1 package (8 ounces) cream cheese, softened
1/2 cup granulated sugar
1 teaspoon almond extract
3 eggs, separated
1/4 cup confectioners sugar
1 cup heavy cream
Grated chocolate and/or whipped cream to decorate

To make crust:
   Preheat oven to 350°. Grease 8-inch springform pan and set aside.
Place graham cracker crumbs, cocoa, and sugar in bowl and stir until well

combined. Pour in butter and stir until well blended. Spoon into spring-form pan and press evenly on bottom. Smooth top. Bake in preheated oven 10 minutes. Cool completely on wire rack.

To make cheesecake:

Melt chocolate in heavy saucepan over low heat. Remove from heat and set aside to cool completely. Sprinkle gelatin over warm milk, stir well, and set aside. Place cream cheese in mixing bowl and beat until fluffy. Beat in granulated sugar and almond extract. Add egg yolks, one at a time, beating well after each addition. Add melted chocolate and gelatin mixture and beat well. Set aside. Wash and dry beaters. Place egg whites in separate mixing bowl and beat until foamy. Add confectioners sugar and beat until stiff peaks form. Fold into reserved chocolate-cheese mixture. Wash beaters again and beat cream until firm. Fold into chocolate-cheese mixture. Pour over crust and smooth top. Refrigerate at least 4 hours or until set.

To serve: Carefully run tip of sharp knife around inside edge of springform pan. Release and remove side of pan. Leave cake on bottom of springform pan and place on serving plate. Decorate cheesecake with grated chocolate and/or whipped cream. 10 to 12 servings

Note: You may substitute chocolate graham cracker crumbs for plain graham cracker crumbs and eliminate cocoa in crust.

Chocolate Roll

5 large eggs, separated
2/3 cup sugar
6 ounces semi-sweet chocolate
3 tablespoons strong coffee
Cocoa
1-1/4 cups heavy cream, whipped

Butter a 12 x 8-inch baking sheet. Line it with waxed paper and butter paper. Beat egg yolks and sugar with a rotary beater or electric mixer until thick and pale in color. Combine chocolate and coffee and place over low heat. Stir until chocolate melts. Let mixture cool slightly, then stir it into egg yolks. Beat egg whites until stiff and fold them in. Spread mixture evenly on prepared baking sheet and bake 15 minutes at 350°, or until a knife inserted in the middle comes out clean. Do not overbake.

Remove pan from oven and cover cake with a damp cloth. Let stand 30 minutes or until cool. Loosen cake from baking sheet and dust cake generously with cocoa. Turn cake out on waxed paper, cocoa side down, and carefully remove paper from bottom of cake. Spread cake with whipped cream, sweetened and flavored to taste, and roll up like a jelly roll. For easy rolling, firmly grasp each corner of waxed paper on which cake was turned out and flip over about two inches of the edge on top of cake. Continue to roll by further lifting waxed paper. The last roll should deposit the log on a long platter. Cover top with whipped cream. Garnish with chocolate shavings and holly sprigs.

8 servings

Quick Brandied Chocolate Treat

1 cup (6 ounces) semisweet chocolate chips
1 tablespoon sugar
2 eggs
2 teaspoons brandy
3/4 cup milk
1 cup heavy cream, whipped

Place chocolate chips, sugar, eggs, and brandy in container of blender and set aside. Place milk in saucepan and heat just until bubbles begin to form around edges. Pour into blender, cover, and blend on high one minute. Pour mixture into 6 custard cups and refrigerate until well chilled, about 2 hours. Top each serving with whipped cream just before serving.

6 servings

Chocolate Soufflé

2 ounces (2 squares) unsweetened chocolate
1 cup milk or half and half
3 tablespoons butter
3 tablespoons all-purpose flour
2/3 cup sugar
2 tablespoons Cognac
1 teaspoon vanilla
1/8 teaspoon salt
4 egg yolks
5 egg whites
Flavored whipped cream

Preheat oven to 400°. Lightly grease 1-1/2-quart soufflé dish and set aside. Place chocolate and milk in heavy saucepan and cook over low heat, stirring until melted and well combined. Set aside. Melt butter in medium-size saucepan. Turn off heat and stir in flour to make smooth paste. Pour chocolate mixture into flour mixture slowly, stirring constantly until smooth. Cook over low heat, stirring constantly until mixture thickens. Stir in sugar, Cognac, vanilla, and salt. Cook about two minutes until sugar is dissolved. Set aside to cool slightly.

Beat egg yolks until creamy. Add 2 to 3 tablespoons chocolate mixture slowly, beating constantly. Pour mixture into remainder of chocolate mixture, beating constantly. Spoon into large mixing bowl and set aside. Beat egg whites until stiff peaks form and fold into chocolate mixture. Gently pour mixture into prepared soufflé dish. Cut strip of aluminum foil long enough to wrap around dish. Fold in half lengthwise and grease on 1 side. Wrap around dish, extending 2 inches above dish, greased surface on inside. Secure with string. Place in preheated oven on lowest rack and bake 40 to 45 minutes until well risen and firm on top. Serve immediately with flavored whipped cream.

6 servings

La Gourmandise Brownies

1 cup lightly salted butter, softened
3 3-ounce bars bittersweet European chocolate, melted and cooled
6 eggs, at room temperature
1-3/4 cups sugar
1/4 teaspoon vanilla
2-1/2 cups all-purpose flour
Confectioners sugar

Use a wire whisk to prepare this entire recipe. Combine butter and melted chocolate. In a separate bowl combine thoroughly the eggs and sugar, but do not overbeat. Stir in vanilla. Add flour, then chocolate mixture, to sugar and eggs. Again, do not overmix. Pour batter into buttered 12 x 8-1/2-inch pan and bake at 300° for 25 to 30 minutes. Do not overbake; these brownies should be soft in the middle. Cool. Dust heavily with confectioners sugar. Refrigerate overnight. Cut into 1-inch squares.

Baked Chocolate Demon

2 cups granulated sugar, divided
2 cups all-purpose flour
2 teaspoons baking powder
1-1/2 teaspoons baking soda
1/4 teaspoon salt
2 ounces (2 squares) unsweetened chocolate
1/4 cup butter
1 cup milk
1/2 cup slivered almonds (optional)
1 teaspoon vanilla
2/3 cup firmly packed brown sugar
6 tablespoons unsweetened cocoa
Flavored whipped cream to serve (see below)

Preheat oven to 350°. Lightly grease 2-1/2-quart round baking dish and set aside. Combine 1-1/3 cups granulated sugar, flour, baking powder, baking soda, and salt. Sift into large mixing bowl and set aside. Melt chocolate and butter in heavy saucepan over low heat, stirring constantly. Add to reserved flour mixture and stir well. Add milk, almonds, and vanilla and stir to smooth batter. Pour batter evenly into prepared baking dish. Sprinkle brown sugar, remaining 2/3 cup granulated sugar, and cocoa on top of batter. Pour 2 cups water over mixture, but DO NOT (!) stir. Bake in preheated oven 1 hour. When done, a crust will have formed on top and chocolate will be runny beneath crust. Serve in dessert bowls, topped with flavored whipped cream.

Note: Heavy cream will double in volume when whipped. For each cup of cream to be whipped, add 2 tablespoons confectioners sugar and 1 to 2 teaspoons vanilla or brandy. Flavoring should be added when cream has just begun to thicken.

10 servings

Halloween Cupcakes

1-1/2 cups self-rising flour
1 teaspoon cinnamon
1 cup sugar
3/4 cup canned pumpkin purée
1/2 cup plus 2 tablespoons vegetable oil
2 eggs
1/2 cup (3 ounces) semisweet chocolate chips
1/2 cup chopped nuts (walnuts or pecans)
Chocolate chips to decorate

Preheat oven to 350°. Place cupcake liners in 18 muffin cups and set aside. Place flour and cinnamon in bowl, stir to combine, and set aside. Place sugar, pumpkin, and vegetable oil in separate large bowl. Beat until thoroughly blended. Add eggs, 1 at a time, beating after each addition. Add flour in small amounts, stirring well after each addition until well blended. Stir in chocolate chips and nuts. Fill lined muffin cups two-thirds full. Place in center of preheated oven and bake 20 to 25 minutes or until tops of cupcakes spring back when pressed gently. Place muffin pans on wire racks and press chocolate chips gently into tops of cupcakes. Cool about 10 minutes and remove from muffin pans.
18 cupcakes

Chocolate Pecan Pie

1-1/2 ounces unsweetened baking chocolate
3 tablespoons butter
3 eggs, lightly beaten
1 cup sugar
1/2 cup corn syrup
1 cup pecans, broken
1 unbaked pie shell

Melt chocolate and butter in double boiler. Cool slightly. Add beaten eggs to chocolate mixture. Then beat in sugar and corn syrup with whisk. Add pecans. Fill unbaked pie shell with mixture and bake for 10 minutes at 400°, then for 30 to 35 minutes at 350°. Serve either cold or hot. Delicious topped with whipped cream.

Cookies

Greetings!

Mix your batter gaily,
Choose a colored bowl;
Make a cheerful clatter,
Whistle as you roll!

The cookies will be better,
The afternoon less long,
If you do your baking
To a tuneful song!

Drop and
Mold Cookies

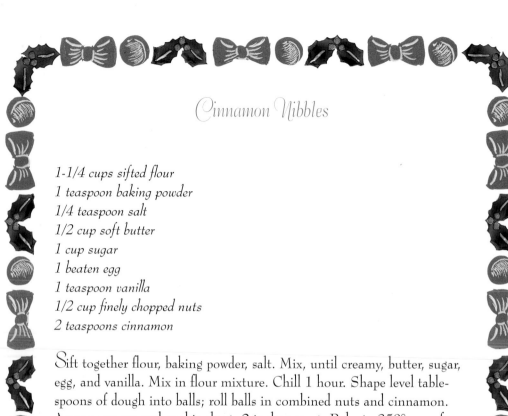

Cinnamon Nibbles

1-1/4 cups sifted flour
1 teaspoon baking powder
1/4 teaspoon salt
1/2 cup soft butter
1 cup sugar
1 beaten egg
1 teaspoon vanilla
1/2 cup finely chopped nuts
2 teaspoons cinnamon

Sift together flour, baking powder, salt. Mix, until creamy, butter, sugar, egg, and vanilla. Mix in flour mixture. Chill 1 hour. Shape level table-spoons of dough into balls; roll balls in combined nuts and cinnamon. Arrange on greased cookie sheet, 2 inches apart. Bake in 350° oven for 12 minutes.

30 cookies

Snow Drops

1 cup soft butter
1/2 cup confectioners sugar (sifted if lumpy)
1/4 teaspoon salt
3/4 cup finely chopped walnuts
2-1/4 cups flour
Confectioners sugar for rolling

Mix first 4 ingredients thoroughly. Work in flour with hands. Chill dough. Roll into balls about 1 inch in diameter. Bake at 350° on ungreased cookie sheets until set—not brown—for about 10-12 minutes. Let stand for an hour to dry. Then roll in confectioners sugar.

40 cookies

Oatmeal Hermits

1-1/2 cups sifted flour
2 teaspoons baking powder
1/2 teaspoon salt
1/2 teaspoon cinnamon
2 cups rolled oats
1 cup raisins
1/2 cup butter
1 cup sugar
2 eggs
1/2 cup milk

Sift together flour, baking powder, salt, and cinnamon; stir in oats and raisins. Cream butter; gradually beat in sugar, then eggs. Stir in flour and oats mixture alternately with milk. Drop from teaspoon on greased baking sheet and bake in 350° oven about 12 minutes.

36 cookies

Kris Kringles

1/2 cup butter
1/4 cup sugar
1 beaten egg yolk
1 tablespoon grated orange peel
1 teaspoon grated lemon peel
1 teaspoon lemon juice
1 cup flour
1/8 teaspoon salt
1 slightly beaten egg white
1/2 cup chopped walnuts
10 candied cherries

Cream butter and sugar; add egg yolk, orange and lemon peel, and lemon juice. Beat thoroughly. Stir in flour and salt. Chill until firm. Form balls about 1/2 inch in diameter. Dip in egg white and roll lightly in nuts. Place on greased cookie sheet; press 1/2 candied cherry in center of each. Bake in 325° oven about 20 minutes.

20 cookies

Old-Fashioned Soft Cookies

2 cups sifted flour
1/2 teaspoon baking soda
1/2 teaspoon salt
1/2 cup soft butter
1 cup sugar
1 egg yolk
1/2 cup buttermilk or sour milk
1/2 teaspoon vanilla
1 egg white

Sift together first 3 ingredients. Mix butter, sugar, and egg yolk until fluffy. Mix in flour mixture alternately with buttermilk; then mix in vanilla. Fold in egg white, beaten stiff. Drop by tablespoonfuls, 3 inches apart, onto greased cookie sheet. Flatten with spatula to 1/2-inch thickness. Bake until golden brown in 350° oven, about 15 minutes.

18 cookies

Rolling Pin
Cookies

Ginger Cookies

1/2 cup shortening
1/2 cup sugar
1/2 cup light molasses
1/2 tablespoon vinegar
1 beaten egg
3 cups all-purpose flour
1/4 teaspoon salt
1/2 teaspoon baking soda
1/2 teaspoon cinnamon
1/2 teaspoon ginger

Bring shortening, sugar, molasses, and vinegar to boil. Cool and add egg. Add sifted dry ingredients; mix well. Shape into roll and chill. Cut into rounds 1/4-inch thick. Bake on greased cookie sheet in 375° oven for 15 minutes.

30 cookies

Sugar Cookies

1/2 cup soft butter
1/2 cup sugar
1 egg
1 tablespoon milk or cream
1/2 teaspoon vanilla
1/2 teaspoon lemon extract
1-1/2 cups flour
1/2 teaspoon baking soda
1/4 teaspoon salt
Colored sugar

Combine ingredients in above order. Chill dough. Roll out very thin, about 1/16-inch thick. Cut into fancy shapes with cookie cutters. Sprinkle with colored sugar and bake at 350° on greased cookie sheets until very lightly browned—about 5 to 6 minutes. Watch carefully to keep from over-browning.

About 80 small cookies

Gingerbread Men

1-1/4 cups sifted flour
3/4 teaspoon baking soda
1/2 teaspoon ginger
1/2 cup molasses
1/4 cup soft butter
1 teaspoon grated orange rind
Raisins and candied fruits for decoration

Sift together first 3 ingredients. Bring molasses and shortening to boil in sauce pan; cool slightly. Add flour mixture and orange rind; mix well. Chill thoroughly. Roll dough to 1/8-inch thickness. Cut with man-shaped cookie cutter. Decorate with small raisins and bits of candied fruits. Bake on greased cookie sheet, 1/2 inch apart, 8 to 10 minutes in 350° oven.

36 men

Brown Sugar Cookies

4 eggs
1 pound brown sugar
1-1/2 cups flour
1-1/2 teaspoons baking powder
1 pinch salt
1/2 teaspoon vanilla
2 cups pecans
Juice of 1/2 lemon

Beat eggs and brown sugar together. Cook in double boiler about 20 minutes, until thick. Combine with remainder of ingredients. Roll dough out, cut in desired shapes, and bake in 350° oven about 20 minutes.

Bars and
Squares

Brownies

2/3 cup sifted flour
1/2 teaspoon baking powder
3/4 teaspoon salt
1 cup sugar
1/2 cup soft butter
2 eggs
1 teaspoon vanilla
2 squares unsweetened chocolate, melted
1 cup chopped walnuts

Sift together first 3 ingredients. Gradually add sugar to butter, mixing until light. Add eggs and vanilla; mix until smooth. Blend in chocolate, then flour mixture and walnuts. Turn into greased pan. Bake in 350° oven 30 minutes. Cool in pan; cut into squares.

16 brownies

Apricot Bars

2/3 cup dried apricots
1/2 cup soft butter
1/4 cup sugar
1-1/3 cups sifted flour, divided
1/2 teaspoon baking powder
1/4 teaspoon salt
1 cup brown sugar
2 well-beaten eggs
1/2 teaspoon vanilla
1/2 cup chopped nuts
Confectioners sugar

Rinse apricots; cover with water; boil 10 minutes. Drain, cool, and chop. Mix, until crumbly, butter, sugar, and 1 cup flour. Pack into greased shallow, square pan. Bake in 350° oven about 8 minutes, or until lightly browned. Sift together remaining 1/3 cup flour, baking powder, and salt. Gradually beat brown sugar into eggs. Add flour mixture; mix well. Mix in vanilla, nuts, apricots. Spread over baked layer. Bake 40 minutes in 350° oven, or until done. Cool in pan; cut into bars; roll in confectioners sugar.

32 bars

Special Gift
Cookies

Brown Lace Cookies

2 cups brown sugar
1/4 cup butter
2 eggs, well beaten
1 teaspoon vanilla
1 teaspoon baking powder
1/2 cup flour
1/2 pound pecans, cut coarse

Cream sugar and butter; add eggs and vanilla. Add baking powder to flour and mix with nuts, and combine the two mixtures. Chill until firm, 1 hour or more.

Drop by 1/2 teaspoonfuls 3 inches apart on buttered and floured cookie sheet. Bake at 350° until golden brown. Remove from pan when slightly cooled.

Viennese Crescents

1 cup soft butter
1/3 cup sugar
2/3 cup chopped almonds
1/4 teaspoon salt
2 cups flour
Confectioners sugar

Mix first 4 ingredients together thoroughly; work in flour with hands. Chill dough. Pull off small pieces of chilled dough and work with hands until pliable but not sticky. Roll between palms into pencil-thick strips and shape into small crescents on ungreased cookie sheets. Bake at 350° until set but not brown (about 12 minutes). Remove from cookie sheets when cooled and roll in confectioners sugar.

75 cookies

Hungarian Rugelach

1 cup soft sweet butter
1/2 pound soft cream cheese
1/4 teaspoon salt
2 cups sifted flour
1 cup chopped walnuts
1/2 cup sugar
1 tablespoon cinnamon

Mix butter, cheese, and salt until creamy. Mix in flour. Shape into 14 balls. Chill overnight. On lightly floured, cloth-covered board, roll each ball into 6-inch circle. Cut each into quarters. Mix nuts, sugar, cinnamon. Drop rounded teaspoonful of nut mixture on each quarter. Pinch edges of dough together, then form into crescents. Place on ungreased cookie sheet. Bake until light brown in a 325° oven for about 12 minutes.

About 50 cookies

Swedish Spritz

1 cup butter
1 cup sugar
1 well-beaten egg
1/4 teaspoon salt
2 teaspoons vanilla
2-1/2 cups flour

Thoroughly cream butter and sugar; add egg, salt, and vanilla. Beat well. Add sifted flour; mix to smooth dough. Force through cookie press, forming various shapes. Or roll, cut out, and emboss. Bake on ungreased cookie sheet, 2 inches apart, in 350° oven until light brown—about 5 to 8 minutes.

If desired, dip ends of each cookie in chocolate frosting.

Bittersweet Frosting

Melt 1-1/2 squares unsweetened chocolate; cool. Boil 3 tablespoons sugar and 2 tablespoons water until sugar is dissolved. Cool. Stir into chocolate. Let stand until thickened.

Pecan Puffs

1/2 cup butter
2 tablespoons sugar
1 cup cake flour, sifted
1 cup pecans, ground

Cream together butter and sugar until light and fluffy. Stir flour and pecans into butter mixture. Roll dough into small balls. Place on greased baking sheet. Bake at 300° for 45 minutes. Roll while hot in confectioners sugar. Cool. Roll again in confectioners sugar.

About 3 dozen puffs

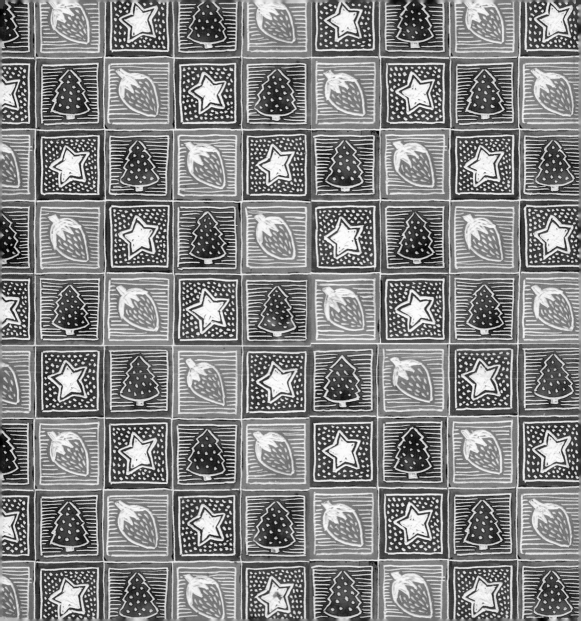